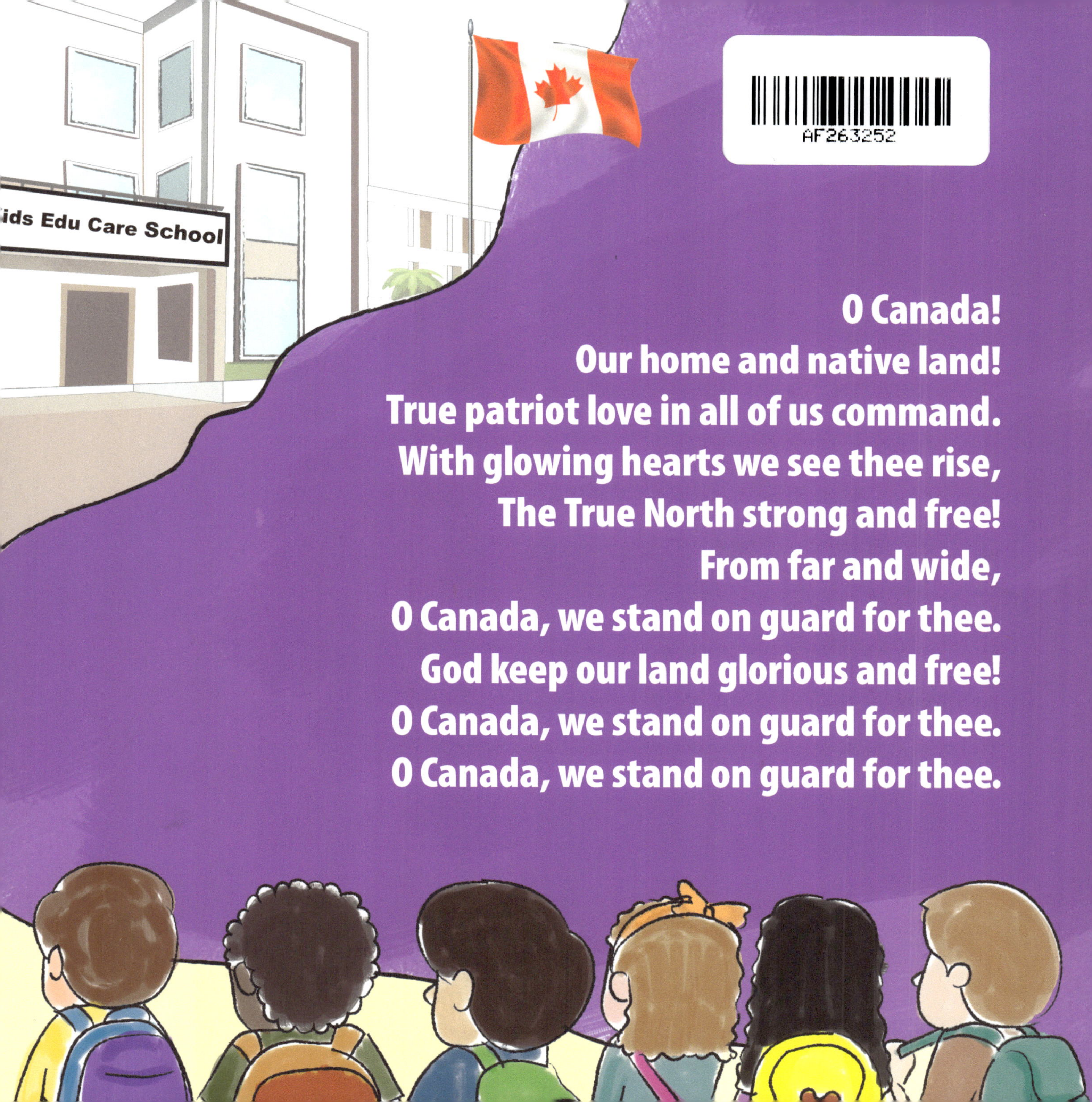
ids Edu Care School
AF263252
O Canada!
Our home and native land!
True patriot love in all of us command.
With glowing hearts we see thee rise,
The True North strong and free!
From far and wide,
O Canada, we stand on guard for thee.
God keep our land glorious and free!
O Canada, we stand on guard for thee.
O Canada, we stand on guard for thee.

THIS BOOK BELONGS TO

We are kids, and our parents, teachers, and elders always advise us to "Work hard and dream big!" I am trying to follow that, but I do not know how I can work hard. How can I dream big? To me, it is unclear what "Work hard and dream big" means...

I am searching and trying to find the meaning of "Work Hard." I work hard at home doing chores. Should I do more? I have dreams when I am sleeping. Should I sleep for longer, so that my dreams will be big?

Yesterday I did a lot of work and then slept all night. I had a dream, but I cannot remember what it was about. I know I have to remember. I have to share, and only then will it make sense.

I want to share and ask my friend about my dream. I believe they can help me with how dreaming big could help me grow and improve myself.

It is a challenge. I started
to work more at home
and sleep early so that I
can dream big. I am also
searching for suggestions
from my friends, and my
mom and dad.

My friend said that I should increase my
school homework, not my home chores.
They also said that dreaming big means I have to
have dreams that make me big.
This is not normal dreaming, though.

My mom always says to work hard and set goals, which would help me to be a good person, but my dad always tells me I have to work hard to be a good student and that I have to have a dream, and only then will I be a success. So, I am confused.

I believe my mom and dad want my success. Both want the same thing, but they use different words and ideas for ways to succeed. However, for a clear understanding, I need more explanation.

Yes, to be successful, we have to work hard. But this does not mean that home chores are the right kind of work. As kids, we need to study in school. All moms and dads expect their kids to succeed, which means we must do our schoolwork and set up goals with a clear vision.

It is tough to be successful without doing well in school. Every day, we need to set aside a few hours for homework to help us succeed in the future. Only then can we move forward toward our dream.

What does "dream" really mean, though? It seems to
have more than one meaning. For one kind of
dream, we have to go to sleep, while another kind
of dream means we must be awake.
There is a difference.

For the second kind, the dream means to set up a vision or goal, and that we must keep that goal in our minds. How do we do that? What are we supposed to like and dislike? Is there any dream in that? What do we want to be in the future?

These are all common questions. But, apart from
that, all kids have dreams. Yes, sometimes small,
and sometimes big, but the reality is,
all kids have dreams.

I am thinking about our childhood dreams. It is a not matter of where we are born or live. No matter where we study, no matter what our skin colour is, or what spiritual beliefs we have, the only thing that matters is what our dream is.

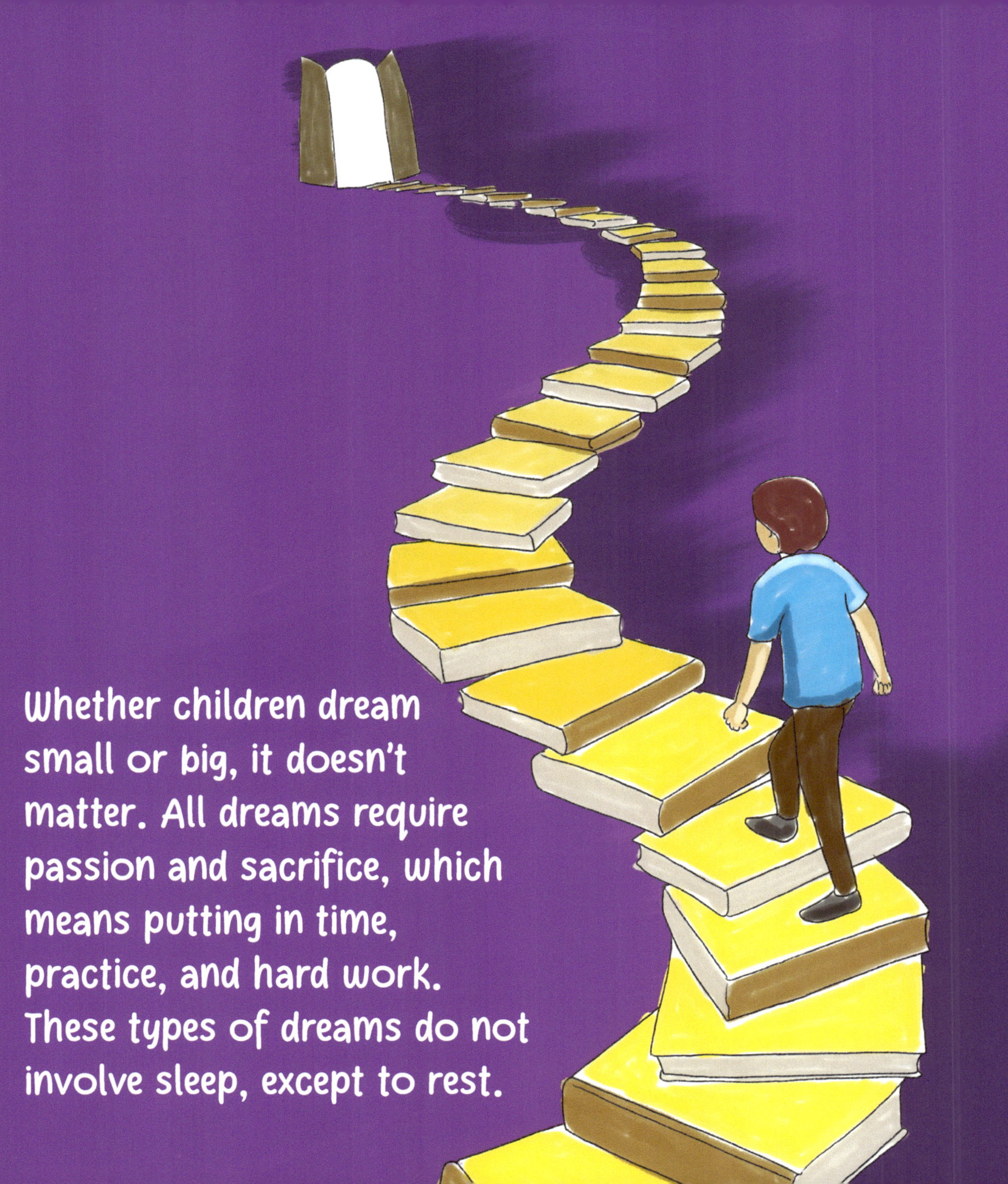

Whether children dream
small or big, it doesn't
matter. All dreams require
passion and sacrifice, which
means putting in time,
practice, and hard work.
These types of dreams do not
involve sleep, except to rest.

These dreams require kids to move forward, and not to stop or give up. This means using our abilities as well as our ideas. But a universal truth is that God created all children with special abilities, no matter what they might be.

Through their dreams, children can create and guide their futures. By focusing on their dreams, they can chart their courses, and hard work will help them reach those dreams.

As long as children work hard and dream big, they can achieve their goals, and no matter how far they go, they will be considered successful.

Working hard will never cause failure,
and along the way, children will gain more and
more experience from their
journey on the road to success. In the end,
God will reward them for their time, energy, and persistence.

If one looks around, one can see proof
in the world that if someone sets their dream big,

and then tries their best and works hard
towards the dream, success can be found that will
sometimes change the whole world.

Work Hard Dream Big

Zabed Mohammad, PhD.
Educator & Researcher
Canada

Edited by
Robert Hart

INFO@KIDSEDUCARE.CA
ZABEDM@KIDSEDUCARE.CA

Library of Congress Cataloging-in-publication Data
ISBN: 978-1-998923-04-5

Publisher: Kids Edu Care Inc.
Children's Dedicated Learning Series
Website: www.kidseducare.ca
Illustration Copyright © 2022 by
Kids Edu Care Inc.

Illustration & Design
Bee Digital

www.ingramcontent.com/pod-product-compliance
Lightning Source LLC
Chambersburg PA
CBHW042204070726

47818CB00036B/376